TEN SILLY ZOMBIES JUMPING ON THE BED

WRITTEN BY
ANTHONY GIANGREGORIO

ILLUSTRATED BY
ANDREW DAWE-COLLINS

Copyright © 2014 by Anthony Giangregorio
ISBN Softcover ISBN 13: 978-1-61199-083-6 ISBN 10: 1-611990-83-1
All rights reserved. No part of this book may be reproduced or transmitted in any form or by any means, electronic or mechanical, including photocopying, recording, or by any information storage and retrieval system, without permission in writing from the copyright owner.
This is a work of fiction. Names, characters, places and incidents either are the product of the author's imagination or are used fictitiously, and any resemblance to any actual persons, living or dead, events, or locales is entirely coincidental.
This book was printed in the United States of America.
For more info on obtaining additional copies of this book, contact:
www.livingdeadpress.com

Ten silly zombies jumping on the bed.

One slipped off . . .

. . . and broke his brain.

Mama called the doctor and the doctor said, "No more zombies jumping on the bed!"

Nine silly zombies
jumping on the bed.

One slipped off . . .

SNAP!

. . . and his arm broke off.

Mama called the doctor and the doctor said, "No more zombies jumping on the bed!"

Eight silly zombies
jumping on the bed.

One slipped off . . .

. . . and snapped his leg.

Mama called the doctor and the doctor said, "No more zombies jumping on the bed!"

Seven silly zombies
jumping on the bed.

One slipped off . . .

. . . and bent in half.

Mama called the doctor and the doctor said, "No more zombies jumping on the bed!"

Six silly zombies jumping on the bed.

One slipped off . . .

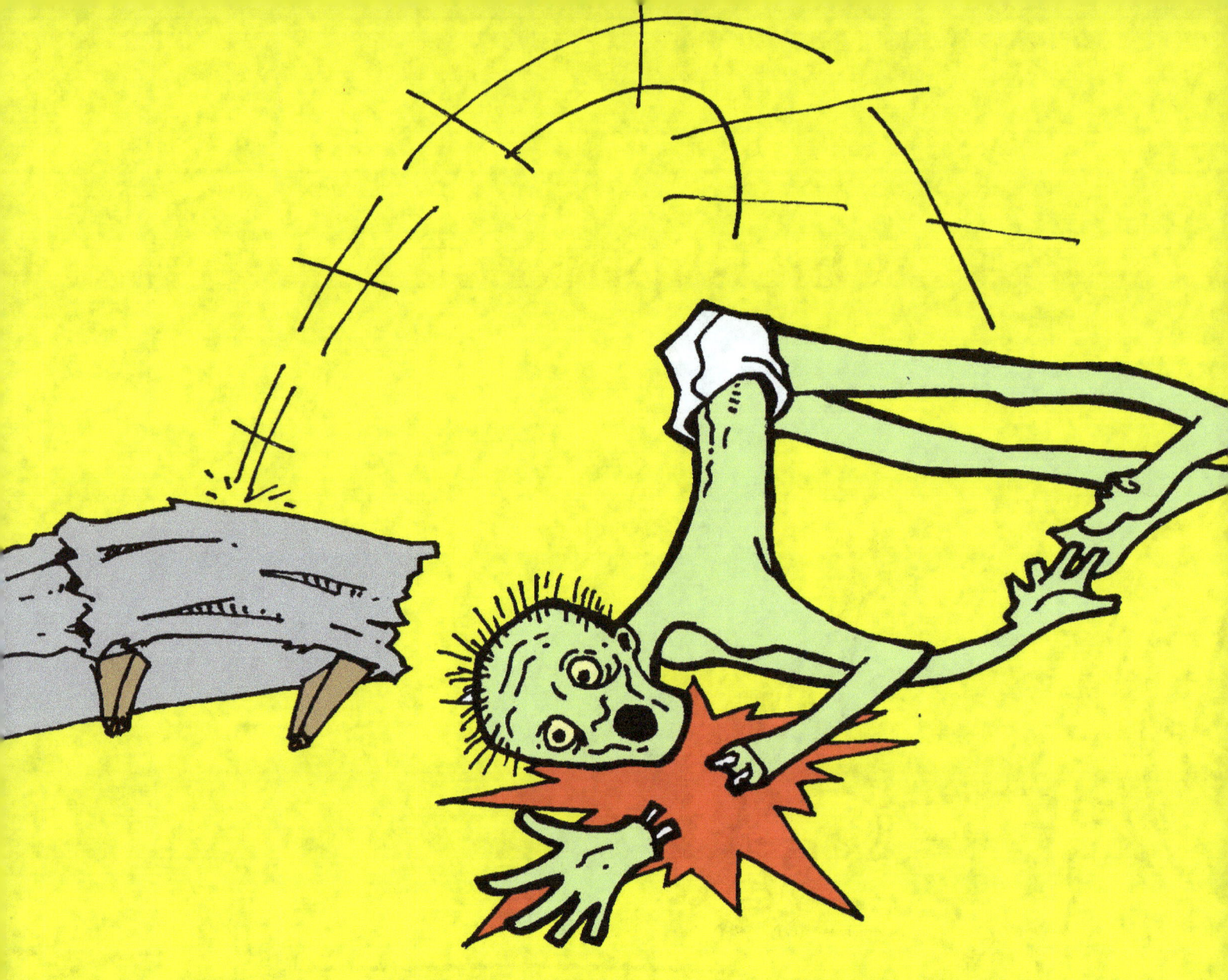

. . . and lost his hand!

Mama called the doctor and the doctor said, "No more zombies jumping on the bed!"

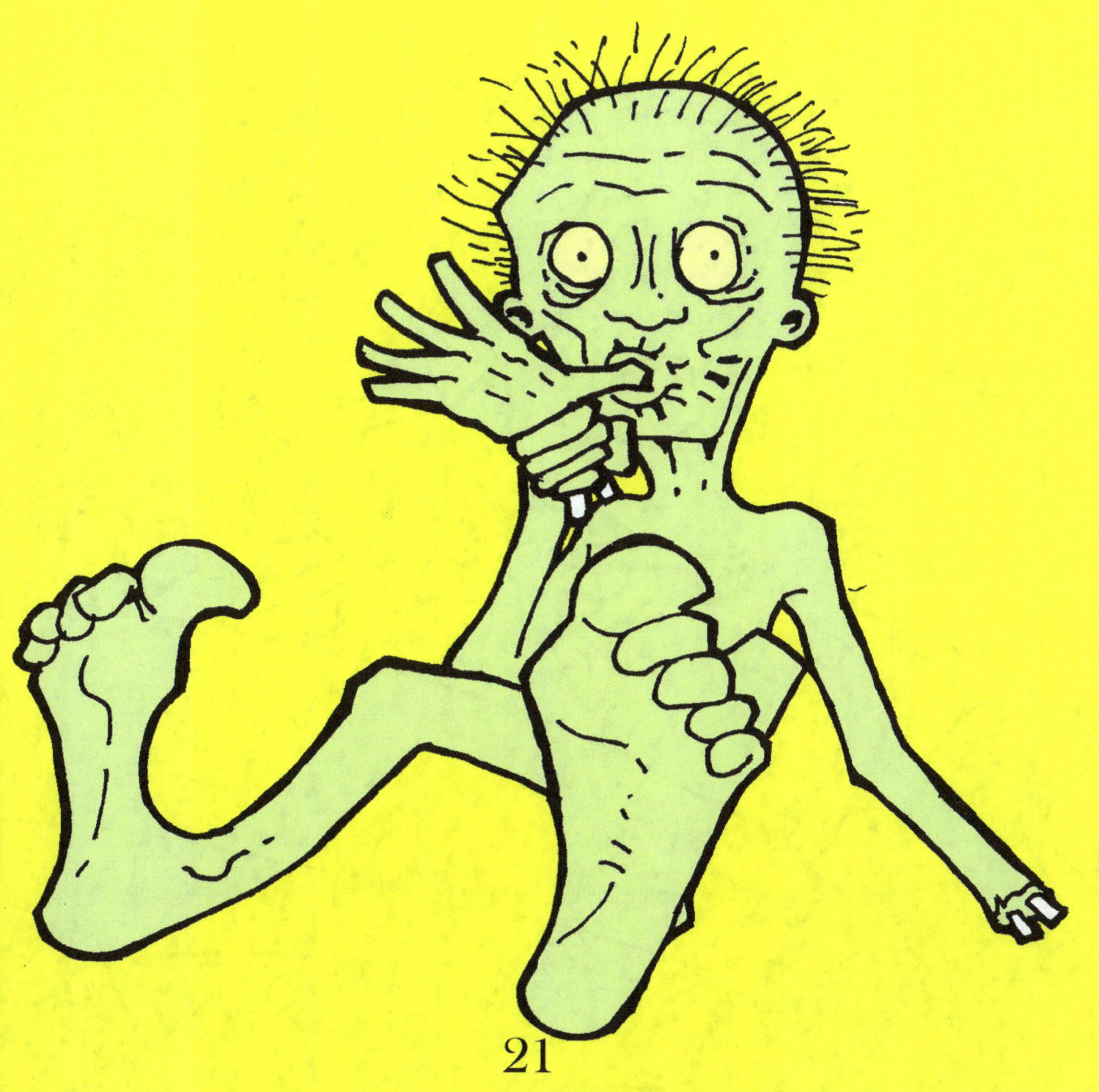

Five silly zombies jumping on the bed.

One slipped off . . .

. . . and lost his limbs.

Mama called the doctor and the doctor said, "No more zombies jumping on the bed!"

Four silly zombies
jumping on the bed.

One slipped off . . .

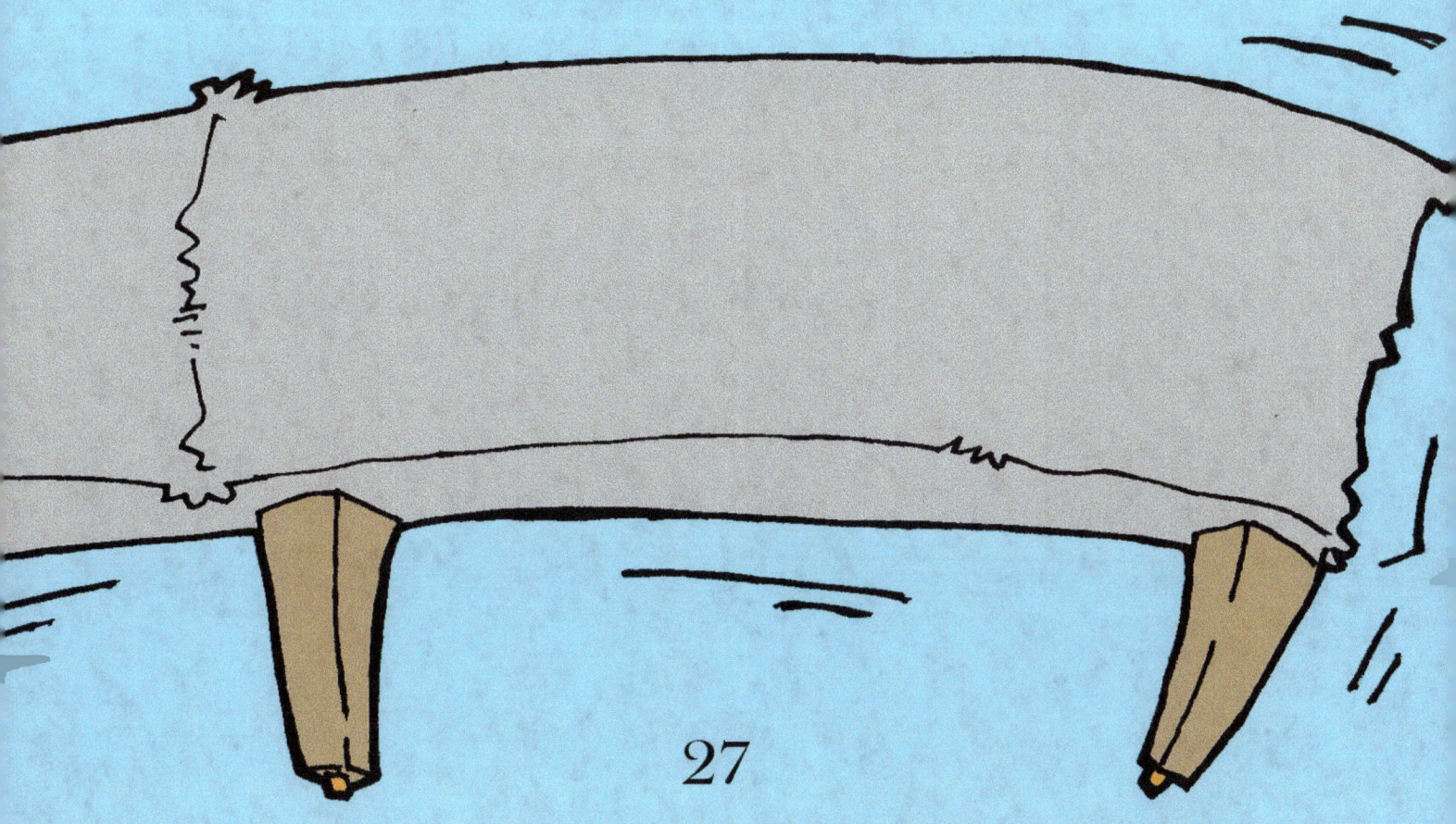

. . . and his eye popped out!

Mama called the doctor and the doctor said, "No more zombies jumping on the bed!"

Three silly zombies jumping on the bed.

One slipped off . . .

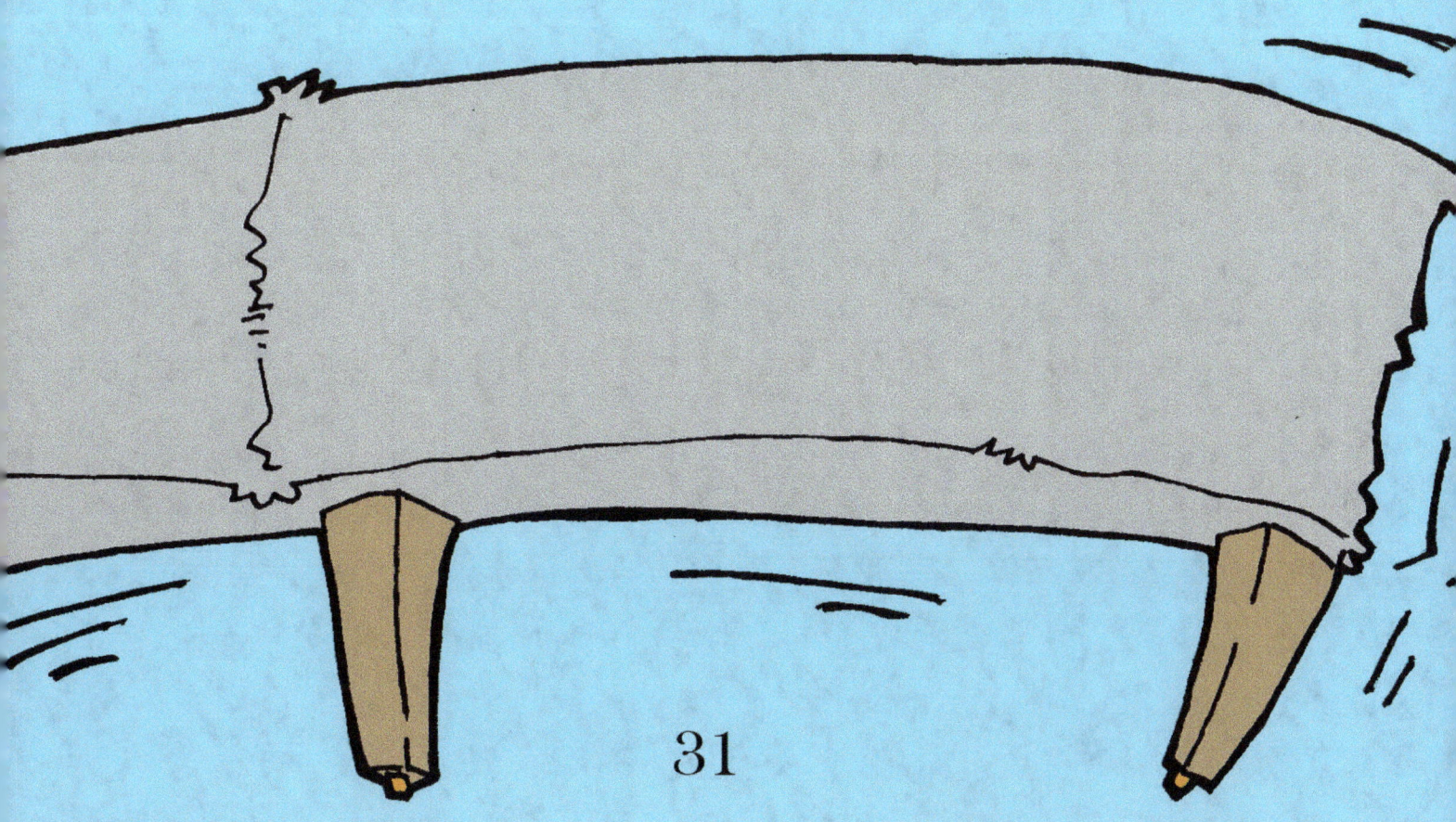

. . . and his heart popped out!

Mama called the doctor and the doctor said, "No more zombies jumping on the bed!"

Two silly zombies jumping on the bed.

One slipped off . . .

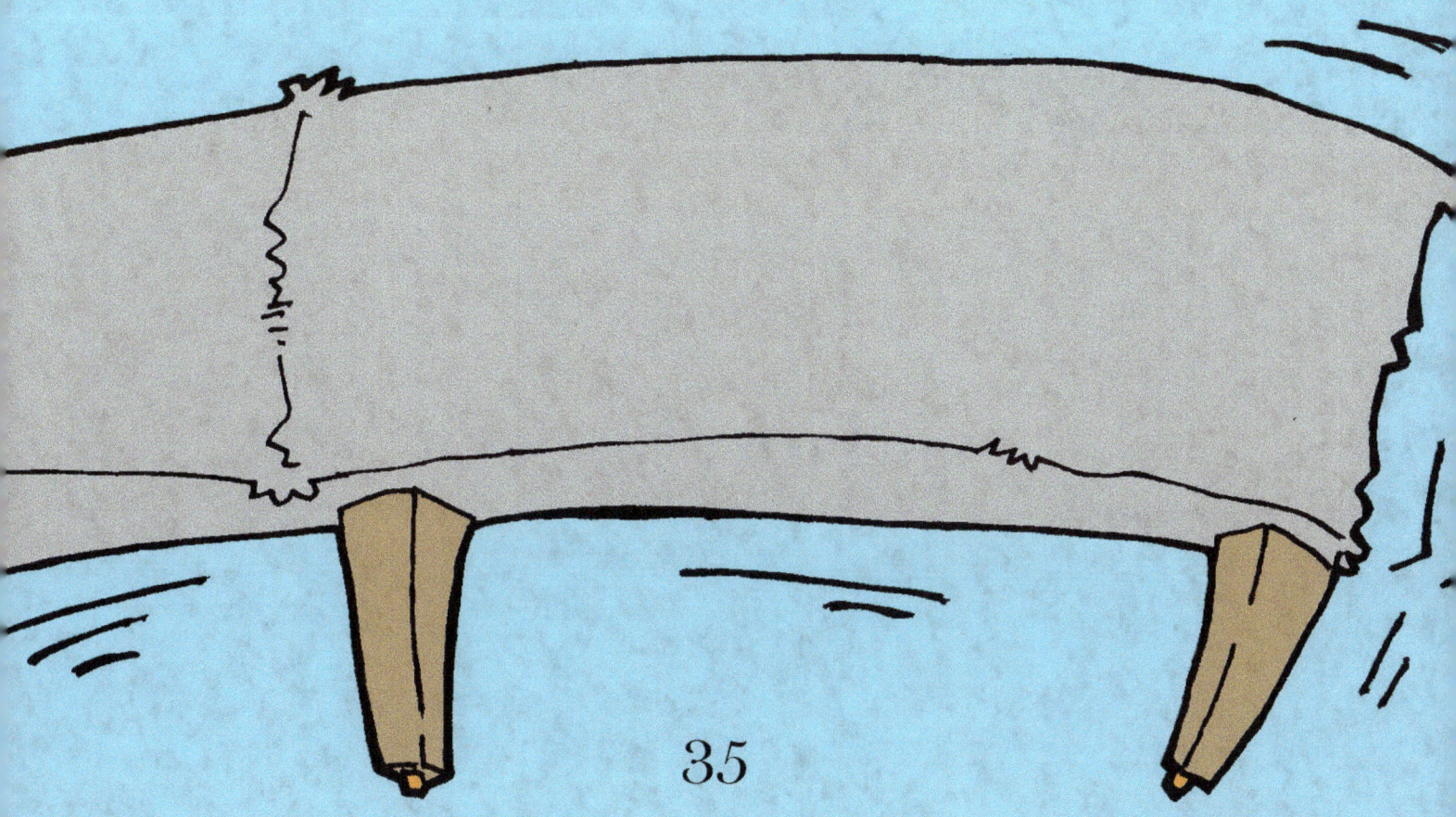

. . . and lost his foot.

Mama called the doctor and the doctor said, "No more zombies jumping on the bed!"

One silly zombie
jumping on the bed.

He slipped off . . .

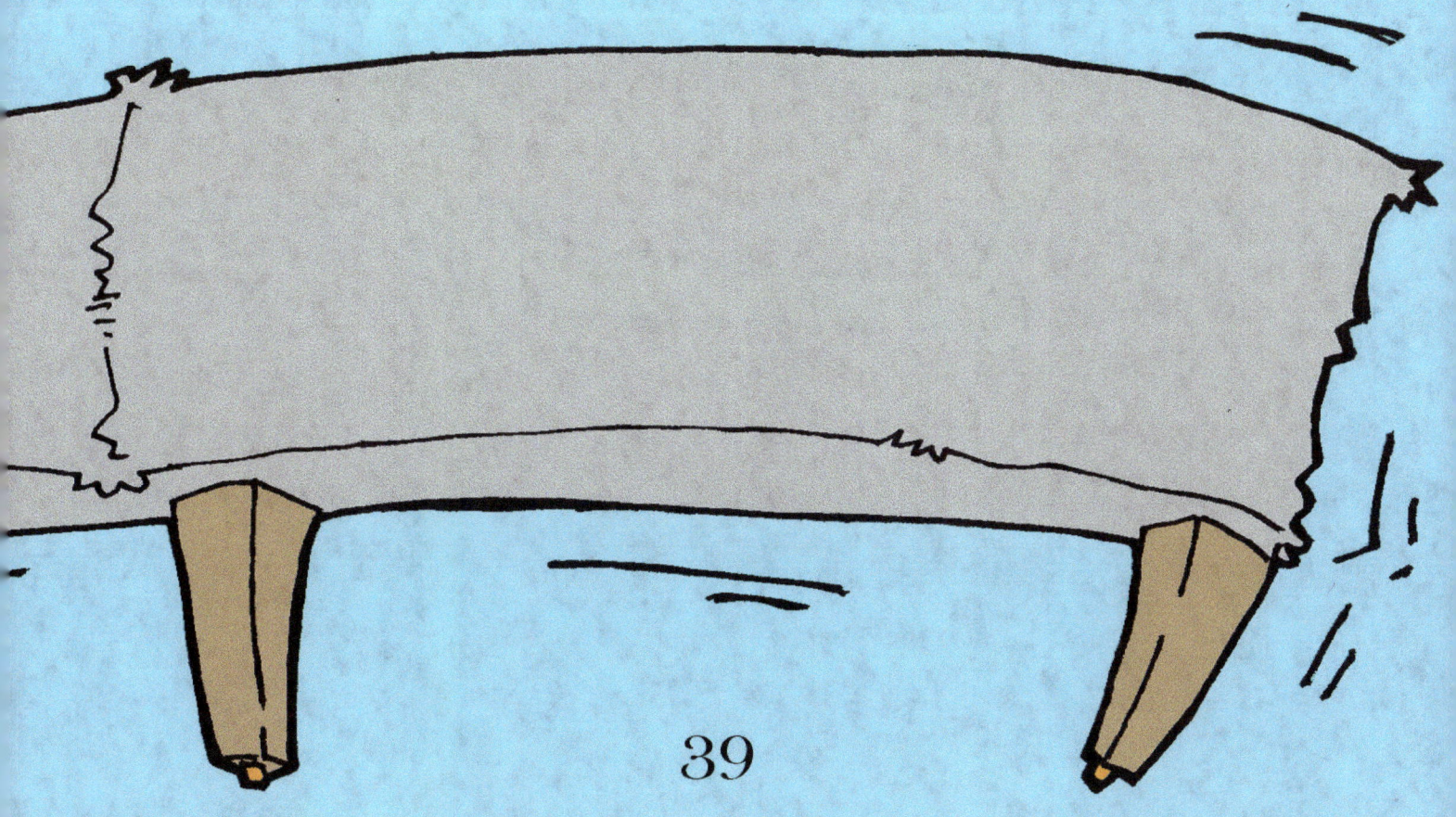

. . . and landed just fine.

Mama called the doctor and the doctor said, "Oh all right, you can have just one zombie jumping on the bed."

ZOMBIES ARE COOL

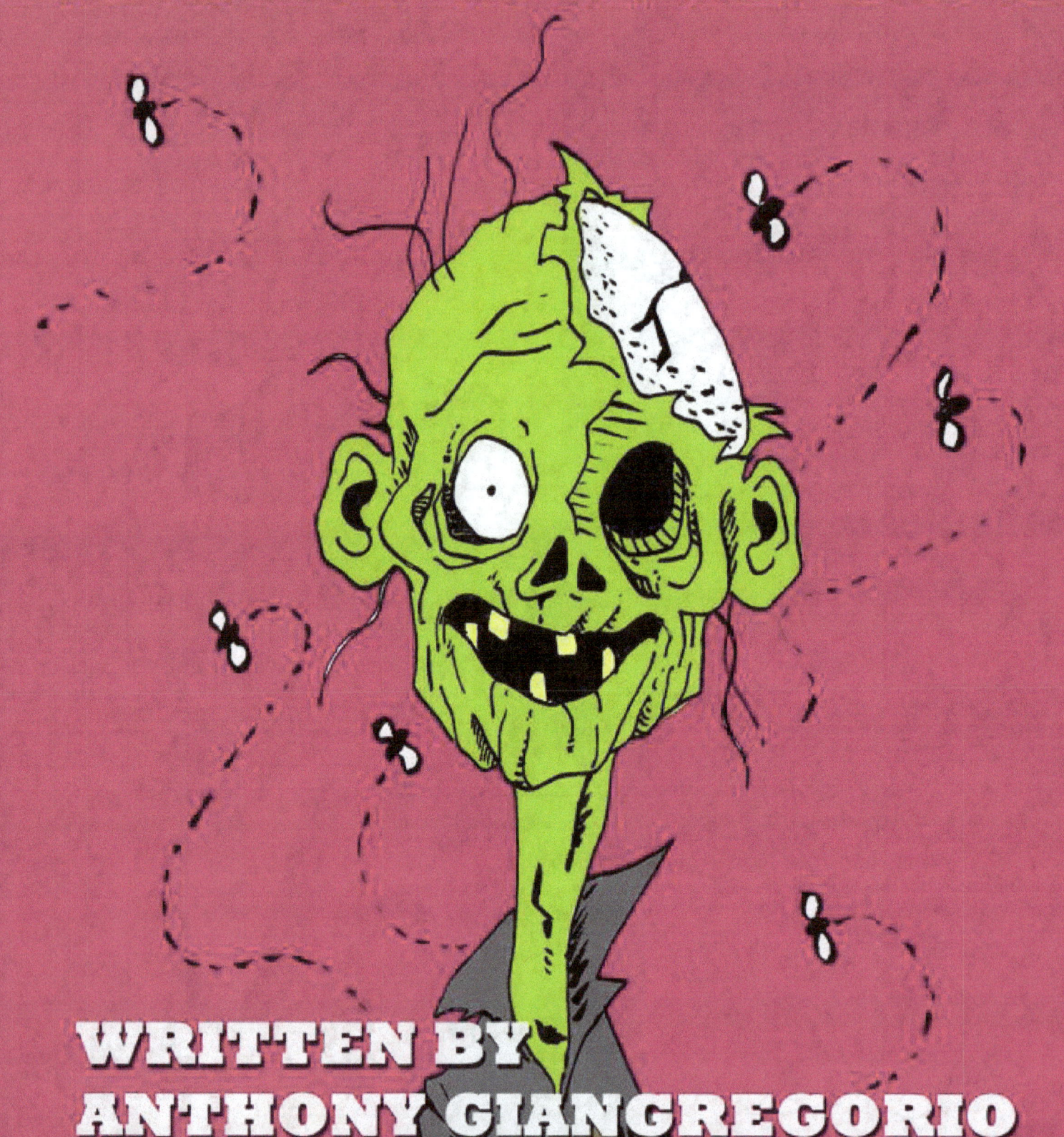

WRITTEN BY
ANTHONY GIANGREGORIO

ILLUSTRATED BY
ANDREW DAWE-COLLINS

www.ingramcontent.com/pod-product-compliance
Lightning Source LLC
Chambersburg PA
CBHW051426070526
44584CB00023B/3605